SHREWSBURY
THROUGH TIME II

MICHAEL PERNA, JR.

AMERICA
THROUGH TIME®
ADDING COLOR TO AMERICAN HISTORY

America Through Time is an imprint of Fonthill Media LLC
www.through-time.com
office@through-time.com

Published by Arcadia Publishing by arrangement with Fonthill Media LLC
For all general information, please contact Arcadia Publishing:
Telephone: 843-853-2070
Fax: 843-853-0044
E-mail: sales@arcadiapublishing.com
For customer service and orders:
Toll-Free 1-888-313-2665

www.arcadiapublishing.com

First published 2019

ISBN 978-1-63500-098-6

Typeset in Mrs Eaves XL Serif Narrow
Printed and bound in England

Foreword

The writing of *Shrewsbury Through Time II* has been nothing if not a labor of love—documenting the history of Shrewsbury and Lake Quinsigamond has developed into a passion over the past thirty-plus years, and it continues to grow as time goes by. My four grandchildren—Tyler, Katlyn, Anthony, and Jack—were included in various phases of the process, including voting on proposed cover photographs, taking photographs of modern-day scenes, and transcribing captions. I have to acknowledge several people who provided valuable support during the writing process: Mr. Frank Morrill and the Harlow family were gracious in allowing the use of their old photographs of various scenes; and Michael Paika, once again, was nice enough to provide "waterborne support" for obtaining views of Lake Quinsigamond. I would also be remiss not to mention the support shown by my fellow members of the Shrewsbury Historical Commission, members of the Shrewsbury Historic District Commission, Shrewsbury Historical Society, and any number of town officials. As a side note, I must mention that I have taken the liberty of including a number of views from around Lake Quinsigamond that, although located on the Worcester side of the lake, involved activities that were an integral part of life in Shrewsbury many years ago. *Shrewsbury Through Time II* will continue the important work of preserving the history of the town and area around Lake Quinsigamond for future generations.

BRODY'S: What originally started off as "Barbeque Bill's," at the corner of Rt. 20 and Grafton St., later became the "Pastrami Shack" for many years. In more recent times, it was transformed into "Brody's," a popular spot for locals and famous people as well, including Jerry Seinfeld, the Governor of Massachusetts, and so on. Brody's continues in operation to this day.

THE WHITE CITY THEATER: The White City Theater opened in the then new White City Plaza in the mid-1960s. It became an immediate attraction throughout the area. After a number of years of being a single-screen operation, the theater was changed to a two-screen layout, with the upper portion, which used to be the balcony seats, being remodeled to a separate area, so two different movies could be shown at once. The theater closed in 2001 and was then torn down. It was replaced by a Bugaboo Creek restaurant, which subsequently also closed. It was then replaced by Jimmy's Tavern, which is a popular destination as of today.

REGATTA POINT: The area just north of the Rt. 9 Bridge, on the Worcester shore, has long been a popular spot for lakeside recreation. Years ago, a women's bath house was located here, along with spots for swimming, fishing, and other lake activities. It became a prime location for watching the regattas that took place every year. In the mid-1950s, Regatta Point became a reality, with modern facilities to store racing shells and sailboats, a snack bar, office area, and a large, sandy beach. To this day, Regatta Point is a central point for Lake Quinsigamond activities of all types.

THE LIBRARY AND CENTER SCHOOL: The photograph above was taken by Herbert Buxton, who not only ran a store in the center of town for many years, but also produced a series of photo postcards detailing scenes around Shrewsbury. As can be seen, the same view today is much different. The Center School that stood right behind the town hall is long gone. The older view does not appear that it was taken from ground level—perhaps it was taken from the roof of the old Cushing-Haven Tavern that stood just across Main Street at the time. Today, the west wing of the modern library building occupies part of the site, along with a granite veteran's monument.

THE BOSTON TURNPIKE: While not particularly noteworthy in a historical sense, the small house that still stands at Boston Turnpike is nonetheless unique. It was built before Rt. 9 was built in the early 1930s, complete with the interesting cupola structure on the roof. Shown in the top view, we can see that the house was right at grade level with the old Boston–Worcester Turnpike. When Rt. 9 was built, the level of the road was raised roughly 30 feet so that the house, owned for many years by the Holden family, now sits well below the highway.

THE TATASSIT CANOE CLUB: In 1891, the then new Tatassit Canoe Club decided to have a club building erected on what was then known as Plum Island, just offshore on what would later become South Quinsigamond Avenue. The building was a beautiful structure, as shown above, with two floors, windows that offered great views of the lake from all angles, and a stained-glass window featuring the club's logo of a sunflower face. The upper level also featured a bar and stage, where the club gave elaborate shows. By 1928, the club was closing. The property, which would become known as Tatassit Beach, was bought by Felix Pollett, who ran the beach until 1975. It was then sold and went through a number of owners before closing for good. The clubhouse itself was burned to the ground in a huge fire in 2009. Today the beach and island are privately owned, with a small cabana occupying the island site. Note the misspelling of the club's name on the postcard!

THE CORNER OF PLAINFIELD AVENUE AND ROUTE 9: The Turnpike Pharmacy opened in 1959 in the building at the corner of Plainfield Avenue and Rt. 9. Prior to this, the location was home to John's Barber Shop for many years. Arthur Atella, shown here in his pharmacist's smock outside the building, operated the pharmacy successfully for many years until it closed. The building was then occupied by a liquor store, followed by a sign business, until it was reopened as Turnpike Liquors in 2013, which continues to operate there today.

MOTELS IN SHREWSBURY: With the increase in families owning automobiles in the 1950s, there was a surge in building motels to accommodate the people travelling from place to place. One of these was the Shrewsbury Motor Inn, which stood at the intersection of Rt. 9 and Elm Street. The operation consisted of a number of parts, including small cottages in the rear of the property, a banquet/dance hall used for functions, other motel units in a larger building, and a bar called the Knight's Lounge. It later was renamed the Tudor Motor Inn. By the 1990s, business had dropped off and the Tudor was closed. Within a few years, the property was bought and the buildings torn down. The Patrick Subaru auto dealership occupies the location today.

EDGEWATER AVENUE BUSINESSES: For many years, a small building that stood at the corner of what is now Edgewater Avenue and Rt. 9 housed Aubain's blacksmith shop. As the years progressed, of course, the need for blacksmith services grew less and less, although the family did do some auto repairs for a time. By the early 1950s, the business closed and the building was sold to the Thomas family, who owned the auto parts business right next door. A number of other businesses operated in the same spot, including a shoe store, leather goods store, bicycle shop, mattress store, and a frame store, until the Sach's Jewelers business moved in. The building has been greatly modified and modernized, with the jewelry business still operating there.

LAKE QUINSIGAMOND BRIDGES: The spot where the current Burns Bridge crosses Lake Quinsigamond has been used to pass from Shrewsbury to Worcester since the early 1800s, when a series of floating bridges were built there. Eventually, during the Civil War years, a dirt causeway, shown here, replaced the bridges. There was only one small passage, between Ramshorn Island and the Worcester shore, which allowed boats and steamboats to pass through. In 1918, the causeway was replaced by a concrete bridge, which, with some improvements over the years, lasted until 2015, when the beautiful, ultra-modern, Kenneth Burns Bridge took its place, as shown in our modern photograph.

MEDICAL FOUNDATIONS: The Worcester Foundation for Experimental Biology was founded in 1944 by Dr. Gregory Pincus and Dr. Hudson Hoagland. The foundation occupied a number of buildings on Maple Avenue. Within a few years, the foundation became known throughout the world as the place where the oral contraceptive pill ("the pill") was developed by Dr. Pincus and Dr. Minh Chueh Chang. Still later, research was conducted by Dr. Chang that pioneered *in vitro* fertilization. By 1997, the foundation was in financial trouble and was taken over by the University of Massachusetts Medical School. It continues in operation today as the Worcester Foundation for Biomedical Research.

HOWIE'S ICE CREAM: Howard Johnson's was built on Rt. 9, at the corner of Harrington Avenue, in the late 1930s, one of many such establishments that existed throughout the country during that era. Run by the Bonin family, "Howie's" became a very popular place, not only for its ice cream, but also as a place to get a good meal. In the 1970s, a nightclub called the Squire's Lounge was added on in the rear of the building and became an instant hit. As the Howard Johnson brand began to fade, the business became known as the Ground Round. It continued on until recent years, when the business and property were sold; today, a Walgreen's Pharmacy occupies the same location.

LEBEAUX'S NURSERY:
The Shrewsbury Nursery business was founded in 1947 by World War II veteran Reuben Lebeaux, shown in the above photograph with the sunglasses on. It was located on the north side of Rt. 9, at the corner of Walnut Street, on land that was originally part of the Lebeaux's family farm, Buttonwood Farm. The business grew and prospered over the years, becoming well known as an excellent source for not only plants, shrubs, and trees of all sorts, but also as a place to get great advice on the care and raising of the same. The business closed in 2009 and the property was unused for a few years until a new nursery-type business was started on the site, and it continues in operation today, with the old nursery business sign still standing.

WORCESTER'S LINCOLN PARK:

Lincoln Park was a very early amusement park, having first opened in the years just after the Civil War. Although it was located in Worcester, just at the west end of the dirt causeway that spanned Lake Quinsigamond at that time, it was a popular attraction for Shrewsbury people. Steamboats ran up and down the lake from the Lincoln Park docks, there were games and later rides of all types, and an outdoor theater provided entertainment. The Worcester and Shrewsbury Railroad carried thousands of patrons down to the park from Union Station, and the Quinsigamond House hotel stood close by (a small footbridge ran over to the park) on Ramshorn Island. By the 1950s, Lincoln Park had just about vanished. The buildings that remained were demolished and today the site is occupied by an elderly high-rise and a high-rise condominium building.

MICKEY'S: This building, built during the 1930s, was originally known as "Dairyland," an ice cream/restaurant operation. It eventually became known as "Mickey Green's," a bar/lounge-type business. "Mickey" Green was a local amateur boxer, who decided to get in to the restaurant/bar business. "Mickey's," as it was popularly known, became a local watering hole from the 1940s to the 1970s. The business then became known as "Joie's" for a number of years until it eventually closed. The building and land were sold and today a car wash is located on the property

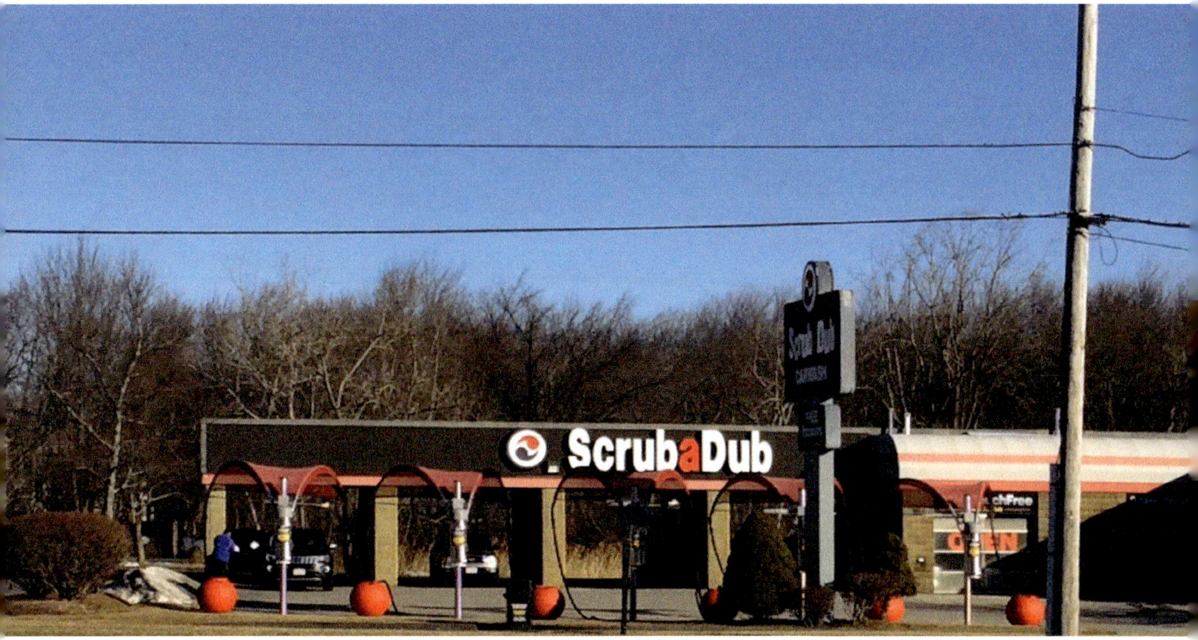

ORLANDO'S MARKET: Opening in 1924 on Rt. 9 at the corner of Edgewater Avenue, the store itself was named after Orlando Orrizzi. The store itself operated on the first floor of the building, with the family itself living upstairs on the second floor. The business was very successful, with many members of the family working in the store. By 1953, the business had grown so prosperous that a new, modern market was built right next door. The family lived in the original house until it was turned into a cleaner business, and still later, a slot-car racing operation. The house was eventually torn down and a bank stands on the site today.

A "Modern" Supermarket: When it opened in 1953, Orlando's Market was the first "modern" supermarket in town. It took the place of the original Orlando's, which operated next door on the first floor of the Orizzi home, Orlando Orizzi being the proprietor. The new store featured a meat department with a number of meat cutters preparing freshly cut meats to order, in addition to a number of other features not found in other markets in town until a number of years later, when an IGA and Big D market came along. After many years of successful operation, Orlando's closed down in 1982. The market building was divided up and has housed a variety of businesses ever since.

THE SHREWSBURY CLUB: When the old Cushing-Haven Tavern was moved to make way for the library, the building was split into a number of sections. The main portion was moved across the street, with several other parts being located at nearby locations. One was moved to West Main Street and used as a dwelling house. In 1902, one of the elderly woman residents knocked over a lamp, resulting in a huge fire that burned the house down. Two women died in the blaze, and it was only with great difficulty that the fire was prevented from burning down most of the center of town, although a few nearby buildings did catch fire also. At the time, it was feared that both the Methodist and Congregational Churches were in danger due to flying embers. Later, the Shrewsbury Club was built on the site. That building, greatly modified, still stands there and has been used as an office building for many years.

THE HARLOW SCHOOL: The Henry Harlow School stood on Holden Street, close to where it meets Rt. 12. The little school was named after Henry Harlow, a veteran of the Civil War who lived nearby. The school served the local neighborhood for many years in the 1930s and '40s then into the 1950s, until it was closed. The school was reopened for a time in the 1960s, when the town's student population outgrew the existing school buildings, before it was finally closed for good. The Harlow School was torn down in 1990 and a small number of town-owned housing units stand on the same site today.

FROSTY'S: For many years, Frosty's was a well-known ice-cream shop that stood just east of Spag's on Rt. 9. Originally, the building was home to a Dairy Queen, but was later added on to and modernized. As opposed to Dairy Queen's menu of mostly soft-serve ice cream, Frosty's offered a wider variety of treats. After serving Shrewsbury residents through the 1980s, Frosty's and a gas station/used car business next door were torn down to make way for a CVS pharmacy, which still stands in that location today.

Dean Park's Flag:

When construction of Dean Park was completed in 1915, it was decided to have a dedication of a "gleaming new flagpole." A ceremony was held on October 27, with both Civil War veterans and the Sons of Union Veterans in attendance. The flag was raised by Grace E. and Bertha Dean, both young girls at the time, followed by all in attendance singing "America." Amazingly, Grace lived until 2013, dying at the age of 105! Today, although the park itself is busier than ever, the flagpole is long gone, with the spot where it was located a quiet little grassy area on the left as one enters the park.

THE CHURCH ON THE COMMON: The First Congregational Church has stood at the head of the common since the earliest days of Shrewsbury. This structure replaced an earlier, much smaller church that was built in 1723. This church building was erected in 1766, and originally stood 50 feet further south and faced to the west. It was moved to its present location in 1834 and turned so that the front of the church faced to the south. The church has been added on to and modernized a number of times over the years—it is still, after all the years, arguably one of the most impressive structures in Shrewsbury.

THE HARRINGTON FAMILY HOUSE: This little house, for many years the home of the Harrington family, still stands at what is now the intersection of Harrington Avenue and Old Mill Road. Old Mill Road, of course, got its name because of the mill that stood just across the road from this house, located on the brook that runs from Old Mill Pond down to Lake Quinsigamond. The house still looks basically the same as years ago, with the exception of the well shown in the above photograph having been removed years ago.

MAPLE AVENUE DINER: This little diner was run by one Tony Frostholm during the 1940s. Mr. Frostholm is remembered for two things: the first was how he would tell customers wearing glasses during the winter that they could avoid their glasses from fogging up as they entered the diner if they walked in backwards; the second is how he made up little photo albums (from which this photograph came) of local scenes and sent them off to people serving in the military during World War II. The location, on Maple Avenue, has housed a pizza shop for many, many years.

The House on Maple Avenue: This house, which still stands on Maple Avenue, just west of the Beal School, was home to John Mason, one of Shrewsbury's gunsmiths. Later on, it was occupied by a group of women school teachers, during the times when female teachers could not be married. We may presume that the ladies in the photograph are some of those teachers. The building, for many years now, has been home to a law office.

MAIN STREET AND GRAFTON STREET STORE: One of the very first stores in town operated out of this building, which stands on the southwest corner of Main Street and Grafton Street. It went through a number of owners over the years, always operating as what we might today describe as a general store, until being changed into the "Center Dairy Bar," which featured a lunch/ice-cream counter, in addition to having other merchandise for sale. It was a well-known gathering place to meet up with neighbors and catch up on the local news. In more recent times, the Dairy Bar closed and the building was transformed into office space, with the exterior being greatly changed.

South Quinsigamond Avenue:

Many people today travelling on South Quinsigamond Avenue often ask questions about the structure shown in our photographs. The strange shape of the building certainly is unusual—it was only during a 1994 telephone call that the story of this Lake Quinsigamond oddity became known. John Adams, whose family owned the complex of homes surrounding this building, related that back in the days before town-owned water service became available, his family had a windmill, which was mounted on the building shown. Water would be pumped from a well into large tanks inside the tower. Gravity would then allow for an early system of running water in the family homes. In addition, water was supplied to several neighbors, including the nearby Washington Club. The "arms" to the windmill and the water tanks were removed long ago, but the tower itself still remains.

THE ESTES BOAT HOUSE: For many years, the group of small buildings shown was home to the Estes family. The Estes family conducted what was, at the time, one of many boat rental businesses scattered around Lake Quinsigamond. In what were somewhat more trusting times, one could stop by, rent a boat and motor, and set out for a day of fishing or just cruising on the lake. Just when Estes Boat House closed is not known, despite inquiring of several long-time Edgemere residents. It certainly was in operation well into the 1960s and probably for some time afterwards. What we do know is that at some point a truck travelling on Rt. 20 went off the road and crashed into the house. Fortunately, as the story is related today, Mr. and Mrs. Estes slept in separate beds on opposite sides of the bedroom—the truck came to rest right in between the beds! Mr. and Mrs. Estes sold the property and moved away shortly after that incident. The building was then home to a real estate business for a number of years. It is now abandoned.

LAKE QUINSIGAMOND CLUBHOUSE: The clubhouse that once stood on a long peninsula at the south end of Lake Quinsigamond was known as the Lithuanian Naturalization and Social Club. What most people do not realize is that, although the peninsula is on the Worcester side of the lake, the site of the club itself is actually part of Shrewsbury, as the "border" is not in a straight line. In more recent years, for reasons unknown today, the club was known as the "Bunny Club." The building later burned, with fire engines from Shrewsbury and Worcester responding, but the club was destroyed. Today, the peninsula is occupied by a number of private residences.

THE ENGLEBREKT CLUB: In this 1963 photograph, we see the Englebrekt Club, a Swedish organization that was a long-lasting presence at 181 Lake Avenue in Worcester. A newspaper article from the summer of 1925 described the club: "The Englebrekt Club, Lake Avenue, is one of the numerous large Swedish clubs at the lake. It is three and a half stories high. It is open each day in the year for members and guests with an experienced chef in attendance at all times. In addition to its home-like atmosphere the club furnishes an ideal place for swimming as there is a large wharf bordering on the lake front." The club existed until 1976, operating as a restaurant and function facility. The building was then taken over by the Marine Corps League. It later burned and was replaced by the modern structure that we see below.

MOREY PLACE: The old home shown in our upper photograph was for many, many years known as the Morey Place. It is said that water for the house was piped down the hill behind it, being obtained from a natural spring. The house itself stood until the Town and Country Bowling Alley (now named Bowlero) was built on the same plot, shown below as it looks today.

TuFran's: For a few years in the early 1950s, the restaurant shown in the top photograph stood at the corner of Rt. 9 and Svenson Road. It was named "TuFran's," which was a combination of parts of the two owner's names—Orlando "Tudor" Orrizzi and Frank Viera. From what some older residents remember, the food at TuFran's was very good, although the business closed after a fairly short time. The building then became home to J. Baker's Shoes for a number of years until eventually it was changed into a bank, which remains in operation today, as shown below.

SLY FAMILY FARM HOUSE: The old farm house shown above was the home of the Nelson Sly family for many, many years. The hill it still stands on today was even known as "Sly's Hill." The old Boston and Worcester Turnpike that runs in front of the house was the scene of a horrific crash between a trolley and an automobile driven by Mr. Sly, in which he was killed. Later, the house became the home of the Chamberlain family, followed by the Moroney family, who started a bookmobile manufacturing business next door. The house still stands and today is rented out as apartments.

NORTH QUINSIGAMOND AVENUE: The corner of Rt. 9 and North Quinsigamond Avenue has been a busy intersection since around the time the White City Amusement Park opened in 1905. In fact, in our photograph above, we can not only see part of a trolley passing by, but part of the roller coaster at the park as well. The building to the right of the view, which we can only see the rear of, was known as "Bill's Diner," one of a number of dining establishments that grew up around the park. Today, the same view looks across busy Rt. 9 to the White City Shopping Plaza.

THE WHITE CITY MARKET: This particular building, as can be seen, was once known as the White City Market. Years later, it became home to Mattero's Bakery, with the family living upstairs above the business. It was well known in town not only for its pastry, but delicious Italian bread and pizzas. The business closed and the building was torn down as part of the development of Quinsigamond Plaza. The entrance to the plaza is right where the building once stood.

THE MASONIC LODGE: This large house, shown in the time prior to 1930, was owned by the Pratt family. Many years later, the building was moved and still stands as a private residence on Maple Avenue, looking very similar to the way it did in this view. After the building was moved, the Matthew John Whittall Lodge of Masons built a brand-new meeting hall on the site, which still stands there today. There was a proposal in recent years to develop a large parcel of land into a multi-use complex, which would have entailed knocking the building down, with the lodge being relocated to a new building, but those plans ultimately fell through.

QUARANTA POST: The house shown here was on the southwest corner of Rt. 9 and Oak Street, owned in 1930 by Walter Penniman and Ruth Eaton. In the years following World War II, it became the quarters of the Victor Quaranta Post 397 of the American Legion. As the membership of the post declined in the 1980s, a decision was made to consolidate the Quaranta Post with the Ray Stone Post, American Legion, and the Charles Murphy Post, Veterans of Foreign Wars. The building was sold and torn down, with a tire store being built in its place.

LAKEVIEW AVENUE HOUSE: Owned by Clara Caulfield in 1930, this house, which stands on the corner of Rt. 9 and Lakeview Avenue, was later converted into a rental property, with an insurance business on the first floor and apartments above. It maintains its basic shape today, although the exterior has been covered with brick. Today, it houses a health/vitamin store and massage business, one of the few remaining structures in the area that was bought up for the Lakeway Commons project.

OLA COTES' HOUSE: This large house, owned by an Ola Cotes in 1930, was located at the corner of Elm Street and Rt. 9. It remained a private residence for many years, but later was vacant for quite some time, before being damaged by a large-scale fire in the late 1960s. The building was torn down, with the land later being developed into a retail/medical building.

THE WEAGLE FAMILY HOUSE AND FARM: This house and farm was owned by the Weagle family at least since the 1920s. Even in to the 1980s, it was not unusual to see flocks of chickens and a few cows roaming the property, even to the point of some of the cows occasionally wandering off to visit the neighbors. The house and associated buildings was sold and torn down to make way for a shopping plaza, which is home to a Staples store, Pier One Imports, and Bed and Bath today.

"DADDY'S FUNKY MUSIC": In 1930, the Eppolito family owned this house on Rt. 9, just west of what would later become Spag's. Later, the Mignacca family lived here for many years. In more recent times, the house was turned into business rental space, being home to "Daddy's Funky Music", where neighborhood kids took music lessons. Still later it was home to a tailor shop, until the building was sold and torn down. The Whole Food market stands on the site today.

GRANGER'S STORE: A neighborhood landmark from at least the 1930s into the 1950s, Granger's Store stood on the northeast corner of Rt. 9 and North Quinsigamond Avenue. Mrs. Jennie Granger was involved in all kinds of things other than running the store—she dealt in real estate, was a Notary Public, and was active in town politics. Attached to the rear of the store was a dance hall named the "Palais Royale," this name being selected when the "town fathers" objected to the proposed name of "Monte Carlo" as being too associated with gambling! Both buildings were later torn down. A muffler shop and a Mexican restaurant operate on this site today.

RAMSHORN ISLAND: Ramshorn Island was connected to the old causeway across Lake Quinsigamond, which was built during the Civil War years. Jesse Johnson (J. J.) Coburn was the first to see the possibilities of creating a resort area around Lake Quinsigamond. He started with a hotel, the Quinsigamond House, on the island, then started running steamboats on the lake. Today, with the new Burns Bridge over the Lake, Ramshorn Island, which was attached to the bridge for so long, became an island once again, with the only access being by boat.

TUCKER'S FARM: Known as the "Tucker Place," this farm stood on the north side of what is today Rt. 20, just west of the intersection with South Street. The Tuckers did not have the best luck—a fire struck the farm at one point, killing two young boys. Later, the place was heavily damaged by a severe storm, possibly a small tornado, which destroyed the barn. The barn was rebuilt in an old-fashioned neighborhood "barn raising." Later, the property was occupied by the Lebeaux brothers, who then went on to develop not only what was called Buttonwood Farm, in the area of Walnut and Fruit Streets, but still later the Shrewsbury Nursery business. The Tucker Place is long gone, with a lumber business standing roughly where the house and barn were years ago.

THE HOUSE ON ELM STREET: This old house, owned for generations by the John Mason family, still stands on what is today Elm Street. The reason the street got that name was because of the "Mason Elm," seen in the older photograph. This tree was identified in the 1894 book *Trees of Worcester* as one of, if not the largest trees in Worcester County. What eventually happened to the tree is not known, but the stately old house remains in the same spot today.

LAKE JUNCTION: This spot, known long ago as "Lake Junction"—a name unknown except to a few local history buffs today—was located on Rt. 9 close to the intersection with Edgewater Avenue. This is where the trolley line split—one branch ran off to the east, paralleling Rt. 9 and continuing on to Boston; the other branch went along the turnpike up to Maple Avenue, then up to the center of town, continuing on through Northborough to Marlborough. In this winter scene, we see a number of local workers clearing snow from the tracks near the small waiting station, with a sign identifying it as Lake Junction on the side of the little building. The same spot today is a great deal busier, with a lot of vehicular traffic passing by at any given moment night or day.

95 Lake Avenue: Organized in 1887, the Lakeside Boat Club's membership was made up mostly of men who worked as clerks in Worcester's offices and banks. The club was very active in promoting rowing activities on Lake Quinsigamond. The clubhouse itself was built on Lake Avenue, just south of what was then Lincoln Park. The clubhouse was later used by the Norton Company as a boathouse and then later served as an armory for the Naval Reserve. The clubhouse still stands at what is now 95 Lake Avenue. It has been used as an apartment building for many years now.

ROMAN CATHOLIC CHURCHES: When the Roman Catholic population in Shrewsbury started to grow, it became apparent that the usual practice of holding Mass services in private homes would not be able to continue. A small chapel, named St. Theresa's, was built on Main Street on land bought from Josiah Stone. The little church served its members well until, once again, it was necessary to have a bigger building. St. Mary's Church, along with St. Anne's Church in the lake section of town, were built in the 1920s and continue to serve their respective parishes to the present day. Little St. Theresa's, for many years now, has been home to a dentist's office.

THE LIBRARY: The building shown here originally stood on the site of what is today the Shrewsbury Public Library. After serving as home to the town's first library, it was moved up Main Street, just west of what became known as "Hale's Block," and was a private residence for a number of years. It then became a restaurant known as "Alcaro's" until it eventually burned down. Today, the Citizen's Bank building, along with a parking lot, occupies the same location.

MONUMENT OF THE CIVIL WAR: The Civil War monument in the center of town was erected in 1869. The names of all the men lost in the Civil War are noted on the monument. The original structure was toppled during a severe ice storm, and a small portion at the top of the monument was broken off, although the monument itself was lifted back into place. The upper photograph shows a group of the local Sons of Union Veterans post in front of the monument. Today, a number of smaller monuments, denoting various historical events, have been relocated to the left and right of the Civil War monument.

CALVIN COOLIDGE SCHOOL: As the population in the lake section of town grew larger, it became apparent that the small Bigelow School, located at the corner of South Quinsigamond Avenue and Ridgeland Road, would have to be replaced by a larger structure. As a result, the Calvin Coolidge School was built in 1928, ironically finished just in time to take over the students from the Bigelow School, which was burned down by a set fire. Coolidge School has served its students well since that time, with a number of additions and improvements over the years, and continues to do so as of this date, now housing kindergarten through grade four.

THE CAUSEWAY: When the Boston–Worcester Turnpike was built in the early 1800s, this "causeway" was used to fill in a low spot in the route. It existed pretty much unchanged, as shown in our older photo when Henry Harlow visited the spot just before the modern Rt. 9 was put in during the early 1930s. Today, Rt. 140 passes beneath Rt. 9 in the same spot. The little brook that has flowed by here since the early days still is able to flow along under the roadway.

ENGINE 1'S HOME: From the late 1920s until the new lake fire station was built in 1951, the little building shown above housed the Shrewsbury Fire Department's equipment for the "lake" area of town. As noted on the sign, this building was home to Engine 1. The firemen for this location consisted of "call" men—part-time firefighters, some of whom (single men at the time) slept at the little station in case of a late night fire. There was no telephone, so any calls from the headquarters at the center of town were placed to the Moalli residence, right in back of the little station, who would then run over and pass along the location of the fire. When the new Lake Station was completed, the old building reverted to private use. It still stands on the site, although modified quite a bit.

THE LITHUANIAN SOCIAL CLUB: Olympia Park was one of the many old ethnic clubs that once stood on the shores of Lake Quinsigamond. Its location, on South Quinsigamond Avenue, was originally home to the "Eyrie Hotel"—one of the very old destinations at the lake. Olympia Park was a Lithuanian social club. It is said that entrance could only be gained by reciting a password phrase in the Lithuanian language. The club itself was still in operation into the 1970s. The property was eventually sold and today the Quinsigamond Shores condominium complex stands on the site.

FAIRLAWN: Ameen Antoun (1888–1976) and his family played a significant part in the development of the Fairlawn section of Shrewsbury. The family lived in a home at the intersection of Maple Avenue and the Boston Turnpike. At one point, the house burned, with the family escaping out a back window. With the creation of several streets with new homes in the area, the Antouns built what would become some of only a few three-story houses in town. Shown above, these houses were located near what is now the intersection of Elm Street and Rt. 9, along with the garages that were built along with them. Today, only one of the houses, shown below, remains. The others were torn down and replaced by gas stations.

THE WITCH'S HOME: This farm on Walnut Street was once home, as the story goes, to Moll Garfield, the "witch," who lived in a small structure behind the main house. Although she was described as a "kind" witch, people still were wary of her. Later the house was added on to, with the same configuration lasting until today, although Moll Garfield is long gone.

BALCH DEAN TAVERN: One of the many taverns that operated on the old Boston–Worcester Turnpike, the Balch Dean tavern was named after the owner of the property, Balch Dean. Mr. Dean was a well-known figure in those days, being very active in town affairs. The tavern was on what was then the main route to get from Shrewsbury to Westborough, today known as Walnut Street. During an epidemic of smallpox, the tavern was used as a hospital for a time. A huge stone arch stood in the cellar, holding up the fireplace. For many years (later in its history), the tavern was owned by the Noonan family, who were living here when this photograph was taken in 1930. The building was demolished, despite efforts to save it, to make way for the Christmas Tree Shop plaza, which stands on the site today.

GARGANIGO FAMILY STORE: The building shown here was built around 1919—it was a combination house/store for the Garganigo family for many years. Minnie Garganigo ran the store for a very long time—the above photograph was taken in 1930—with the store (along with Minnie) operating until at least the early 1980s, in the last few years of operation selling hot dogs and homemade spaghetti sauce. Minnie herself lived until 1989, passing away at the age of ninety-eight. The Garganigo family owned the building for many years afterward, with a tile store operating out of the location until recent years, when the entire area was developed as part of the Quinn 35 development. Albert "Lovey" Garganigo, Minnie's son, still was working part time at the tile store until well in to his late nineties. He passed away in 2016, just shy of his 100th birthday.

DAHL'S "MOM AND POP" STORE: Located at what is now the corner of Dewey Road and Rt. 9, Dahl's Store was a fixture in the Lake neighborhood during the 1930s and later. This was one of many "Mom and Pop" stores scattered throughout the town. Among many other goods, Dahl's featured penny candy and, on the lower, basement level, something more unique—movies for the neighborhood kids with the price of admission being 5 cents for an afternoon of watching the popular *Skippy* movies. The store was run by the Dahl brothers, Ralph and Bill, along with their mother. Some (now elderly) residents remember being sent down to the store to buy cigarettes for their parents—cost: 1 cent each. The top photograph, taken in 1930 prior to the construction of the present-day Rt. 9, shows Dahl's in what was perhaps its heyday. Later on, the property was sold and since the late 1950s has been the site of a White's Cleaners store, with a recent addition of a cell phone repair shop.

105 OAK STREET'S CIDER MILL: Located at what is now 105 Oak Street, this house and attached structure was a cider mill business for many, many years. Originally owned by the Hapgood family, the mill was one of a number in town that produced cider from the thousands of bushels of apples grown in Shrewsbury each year many years ago. Diary entries from Josiah Stone, a life-long resident who was not only a farmer, but very involved in town affairs, tell of bringing wagon after wagon load of apples to the mill to be processed into cider. The 1930 photograph above, when the house/mill was owned by a William Boyce, still has a sign on the attached structure on the left which reads "Cider Mill," although it is not known if the mill was still operating by that date. The house has been a private residence for many years.

SUNSET BEACH: As far back as the 1920s, what is now known as Sunset Beach has been in operation at the South end of Lake Quinsigamond. Originally known as Eckstedt's, the beach was taken over by the Anderson family in 1943. Located on what is now known as Old Faith Road, the beach changed hands again in the 1960s, then being run by the Mulcahy family, Mrs. Mulcahy having been part of the Anderson clan. During the post-World War II years, the beach was known for the huge rubber (government surplus) rafts, from which generations of young swimmers would bounce into the lake. The beach, along with the original old-fashioned snack bar, remains in operation to this day. It has also served as home to the town's summer swimming classes for a number of years.

THE LITTLE BROOK: People passing by this spot today would be hard-pressed to identify it. This 1930 view of the house and property owned for many years by the Iovieno family even shows the little brook that ran down from Old Mill Pond to Lake Quinsigamond, complete with a small bridge crossing it. The house was set back from the Boston–Worcester Turnpike, with a family-run gas station operating close to the highway for many years. In the 1980s, the property was sold, with the house and gas station being torn down. The brook was covered over and the Quinsigamond Plaza built on the site. The location of the house today would be roughly where the Trader Joe's business exists. A running joke at the Verizon store next door is that ducks can sometimes be heard quacking—it could be that they are swimming in the brook running under the building!

ST ANNE'S CEMETERY: Despite many years having passed since the above photograph was taken in 1930, the view looking from this same spot looks surprisingly similar today. The house on the north side of the road is still there. The house on the south side of the road is still there, although now incorporated into a small strip of businesses. St. Anne's cemetery looks more populated with headstones now, with a stone wall along the Turnpike side, but the basic layout and flagpole are about the same. On close examination, we see a workman tending to some task or another in the cemetery. The most noticeable difference, as seen in the bottom photograph, would be the rush of modern vehicles as opposed to the old automobiles and much lighter traffic flow in the top photo. The identification of the property owner, written on the edge of the photograph's negative, states "R. C. Bishop of Springfield." After a bit of confusion initially, the solution dawned—the property at that time was listed as being owned by the Roman Catholic Bishop of Springfield!

DUFRESNE ROOMING HOUSE: For some time after the discovery of this particular view, the location and purpose of the building was a mystery. It was not until a conversation took place with Albert "Lovey" Garganigo, who grew up in the area and at the time was in his late nineties, that it was identified. At first, Lovey said, "Do you see that wall? I used to walk on that wall when I was a kid." With a bit more questioning, he identified the building in the photo as a rooming house, that despite being quite a large structure, did not operate for many years before it was torn down. The names of the owners, listed on the photograph's negative, were Annie and Ella Dufresne—the Dufresnes having owned a number of businesses in the town. Today, a motel stands on the same site.

SPAG'S SUPPLY: Here we have the building that would later become a landmark throughout New England as the home of Spag's Supply. At the time this photograph was taken (1930), the building was owned by Antonio Borgatti, Anthony "Spag" Borgatti's father. The building was vacant and for rent, according to the sign in the window. Once home to a trucking company, this is where Spag would, a few years later, in 1935, start his little hardware, tire, and battery business. As we know now, this business would later grow into a retail success story, a legend in the business world, featured over the years in innumerable newspaper articles, business journals, and a book. The business was eventually closed after the deaths of both Spag and his wife and business partner, Olive. The building 19 chain operated here for a few more years until that closed too. An antiques/flea market occupied the main building for a few more years until the current Quinn 35 development was built, including a Whole Foods Market, Starbucks, many retail and restaurant businesses, and apartments and condominiums. The small monument shown marks the spot and is a tribute to "Spag" and his wife, Olive, complete with a replica of Spag's trademark 10-gallon hat!

Oak Street Bridge: There are probably very few people still around today that would remember what we see in this 1930 photograph, which was taken looking down Oak Street from the corner of Rt. 9. In fact, if not for the state doing a property survey prior to the construction of Rt. 9, we might never have seen a photograph of this particular scene—people back then simply would not have thought to take a picture of it. Just off in the distance can be seen the bridge that allowed Oak Street to pass over the Boston–Worcester trolley tracks. This was one of two bridges—the other being at Walnut Street—that were constructed when the trolley tracks were put in. A few years after this photo was taken, the tracks were taken out, the bridge removed, and the spot filled in so that the road was brought up to the level it is today. The trolley right of way that the bridge spanned is today the driveway to the Sheridan Apartment complex, which can be seen to the right side of the below photograph

OLD GRAFTON STREET AND ROUTE 9: The photograph above shows the intersection of "old" Grafton Street (when you could still cross over Rt. 9) and the Boston–Worcester Turnpike, looking east. The dirt road that was the highway can be seen, along with a traffic signal warning the automobile drivers that would occasionally pass to drive slowly. The house to the left of the view was owned by the Harrington family, who occupied many of the homes in what was then called "South Shrewsbury." It was torn down in later years, the story passed down through the family was that it had to be demolished because squirrels ate away the roof beams! A tire store now stands on the same corner.

THE MITCHELL PLACE: Located on the south side of Spring Street, the Mitchell Place belonged to Joseph T. Mitchell, the son of a Civil War veteran of the Union Army—in fact, he was very active in Andrews Post 135 of the Sons of Union Veterans located in Shrewsbury. The Mitchells were one of the first Roman Catholic families in town. The family had three daughters, Margaret, Helen, and Charlotte. Margaret and Helen both were long-time town employees—neither ever married and they lived on the old homestead. Charlotte served in the military during World War II, later marrying and moving out of town. The Mitchell Place, shown above, looked pretty much the same until the day it was torn down in fairly recent times. The farm was sold after the deaths of Margaret and Helen, making way for a large number of modern houses.

FERRANTE FAMILY HOME: The photograph above was one of the series taken just prior to Rt. 9 being constructed. It is identified as the home of Giovanni Ferrante, with the photograph being dated October 25, 1930. This house still stands at the corner of Rt. 9 and Dewey Road, having still been owned until recent times by the Ferrante family. In recent years, the house has been home to the Simon Jewelers business, as shown below. It would be interesting to know the identities of the young children standing in the doorway when this photograph was taken!

THE STORE ON MAIN STREET: The small building located just east of the town center on Main Street started off as a private residence. By the 1950s, it had become home to a "Clover Farms Store," the Town Fruit store, and Mickey's Shoe Repair. Years later, the building became home to the "Shropshire Shop," which featured collectibles. That business was replaced in recent times by the Shrewsbury Country Shoppe, a gift shop store.

LOVEY'S GARAGE: The Turnpike Garage was one of several that operated along Rt. 9 on the stretch between the Lake Quinsigamond Bridge and Fairlawn. Owned by the Garganigo family, it was later superseded by "Lovey's Garage," operated by Albert "Lovey" Garganigo. "Lovey's" was in business at the same location until the Lakeway Commons project came along, but is still in operation at another location in town

THE STATE POLICE ON ROUTE 9: In what is a very rare view, here we have a group of Massachusetts State Policemen, mounted on horses, along the dirt road that later became Rt. 9. We might speculate that they had stopped here in the days just as Rt. 9 was being built, when a small café named "Moosehead Lodge" was opened just across the road from where they are standing. Today, the Christmas Tree Plaza occupies the area just behind the policemen.

THE ANIMAL HOSPITAL: This house was owned by one Maybelle Pratt in 1930. A few years later, it was bought by a Dr. Shaw, who opened the Shrewsbury Animal Hospital just across the road. The business grew and Dr. Shaw hired another veterinarian to work with him. Dr. Maker, who was the newly hired vet, ended up marrying Dr. Shaw's daughter. The business continued for many years until the property was sold. The buildings were torn down and a number of automobile dealerships occupy this area today.

MOVING HOUSE: This house was built by John Boyd around 1840, but possibly as early as 1815. It was owned by Lyman Newton for many years and stood in the center of town, on the spot where the Hale Drug business moved across Main Street, where the Rite Aid pharmacy now stands. The house was moved in 1968 to its current location at 64 Main Circle. Amazingly, it only took one day to have the house jacked up off its foundation and moved down Main Street to the new location. The "savior" of this old house was Mr. George Munro, who was then president of Munroe Associates. He took an interest in the old house and, along with his wife, spent countless hours restoring it to close to its original form.

MACADAMIZED ROADS: Today, Shrewsbury has mile upon mile of well-paved roads and highways. There are still a few unpaved roads scattered around the town, but these are typically very short in length. This is quite a contrast to a time not long ago when almost all the roads in town were not paved at all. In fact, as recently (perhaps even later) as 1917, there were only three "macadamized" (in other words, paved) roads in town: Main Street, Maple Avenue, and a portion of what is now Rt. 9. It was not until the "modern" Rt. 9 took the place of the old Boston–Worcester Turnpike in the early 1930s that the rest of the road was paved and then eventually became the modern highway it is today. The above view shows the older version of the Turnpike, looking west from the area near Lake Street, the view below shows the same scene today.